D0942636

High on a Windy Hill

ECTOR COUNTY LIBRARY
321 W. 5th St.
Odessa, Texas 79761

MARGERY EVANS ELDRIDGE

EAKIN PRESS ✦ Austin, Texas

FIRST EDITION
Copyright © 2000
By Margery Eldridge
Published in the United States of America
By Eakin Press
A Division of Sunbelt Media, Inc.
P.O. Drawer 90159 ☐ Austin, Texas 78709-0159
email: eakinpub@sig.net
☐ website: www.eakinpress.com ☐
ALL RIGHTS RESERVED.
1   2   3   4   5   6   7   8   9
1-57168-000-0

For CIP information, please access:
www.loc.gov

Dedication

To the three of us.
To my sister,
who became my mother.
To "Pappy."
To my family,
especially my girls,
Lisa, Kimmy, Julie, Emily, Meridith,
who listened to these stories
all of their lives.
To Bob,
who loves and encourages me.
To all "The Little Woodmen,"
especially "Mick."
To my friends and teachers.
To my adoptive parents,
for adopting a 15-year-old,
and
to all the people in Sherman, Texas,
who were always wonderful to
the kids on the hill.

"You may outgrow almost everything else in your life, but never your childhood."

—*Unknown*

Contents

Author's Note

Fictitious names are used throughout this book, including on all photo captions, for privacy reasons. Events portrayed are based on actual facts, with some license taken by the author to create a more interesting read.

Maggie (one), Estelle (four), and Alex (seven).

CHAPTER 1

We Three

Maggie peered through the chained and locked gate guarding a group of crumbling red brick buildings that used to be her home. The real estate man she was to meet was late, so she decided to get out of her car and do some exploring.

She shook the chain to make sure it was really locked. Maggie was never one to take things at face value. It was locked. She leaned over the chain and could almost smell the fragrance of lilacs that were once banked there. They were always the very first sign of spring, and the thing visitors saw as they entered the gate.

She, her sister, Estelle, and her brother, Alex, had first entered this gate in 1931. They were driven from a little West Texas town called Ralls to this North Texas town of Sherman by Alex's teacher, Miss Clark. It had been a long and hot drive, and the cool green expanse of lawns looked inviting. All Maggie knew was that they were going to live in a new home that was known as an orphanage. She did not even know what that word meant. Brother and Sister did.

The big red brick buildings had looked pretty to Maggie.

1

She could not understand why Brother's eyes looked so sad and tears were running down Sister's pale, freckled face. Miss Clark parked the car and told the children to wait until she went to the office to talk to her friend who was secretary to the superintendent. Maggie was so excited that she kept jumping from window to window.

"Is this where we are going to live? Is this like a big school? It sure doesn't look like Granddad's house!" Her eyes were big and brown and danced with excitement.

"No honey," said Brother in a soft voice. "It isn't a school. These are buildings with lots of rooms where boys and girls live who don't have a mother or daddy. It's called an orphanage."

"Will we all three stay together in one room?" Maggie asked hopefully.

"We'll just have to wait and see. But I think you and your sister will stay together, and I will probably stay with some boys." As he said this, he took each of their hands and squeezed. "I won't be far away, and I will see you often, I promise." He swallowed to try to get rid of the lump in his throat. "Let's make this into a great, exciting adventure, and be cheerful when Miss Clark gets back."

"OK! I will! Won't this be fun, Sister?"

"I guess so," her sister answered, wiping away the tears that had streaked her face.

About that time Miss Clark came down the steps from the main building, and she was smiling.

"Let's get your suitcase, girls, and Alex, your box. Just wait until you see your new home. It is so lovely." Alex couldn't be sure, but it looked like she had tears in her eyes.

Maggie was brought back to the present when the young real estate man came flying up the driveway in a sporty BMW. He waved and then jumped out of his car, saying he was sorry to be late. As he unlocked the chain and pulled it aside for her to enter, he told her to drive on up to the main building, which all the kids had called the Big Building. She asked if he minded

2

just leaving the keys to the two buildings, as several of the exes who used to live there were meeting to discuss the future of the old dilapidated buildings. He agreed and asked that she return the keys to his office in town. He then took off in a swirl of dust and gravel. Maggie shook her head as she got out of her car to see if the key to the main door worked. It did, and she pushed the huge solid oak door with glass panels on either side open a crack, but decided to sit on the top step until someone else came. She remembered the first time she, Estelle, and Alex walked up those steep steps. She was back again in her memories, to that hot June day in 1931 when she was six, Sister was nine, and Brother was twelve. . .

Miss Clark introduced the three children to her friend, Miss Lacey, and she smiled at the children and asked them to sit down while she filled out some papers. While Brother answered her questions, Maggie and Estelle looked around the great entry hall. There was a marble fireplace with a huge picture of a lady above it. She was dressed in a long blue lace gown with a diamond pin at the neck. She looked like a queen, but they were told later that she was the president of the Woodmen Circle Insurance Company. Brother told his sisters this was the insurance their mother had bought, and that is why they could come there to live. Maggie knew in her heart she would rather have her mother back, but since she was an angel in heaven, that was out. So Maggie smiled and looked around some more.

There was a really tall chest in the corner with a huge clock in the top. Sister whispered to Maggie that it was a Grandfather Clock and not to be afraid when it bonged the time each hour. On the opposite wall was the most enormous black piano, which Sister quietly told her was a grand piano. Maggie thought it surely *was* a grand piano! She closed her eyes and pretended she was playing it.

She came back suddenly when a tall man with glasses came from another room, which she found out later was the office. He had been making a telephone call to the national office in Omaha, Nebraska, and the three siblings had been accepted. Brother told his sisters later that they were lucky because the insurance policy had lapsed, and they could have been turned away. He also thought that because not only their mother but also their aunt, grandfather and grandmother had died within a year, they were accepted. Brother told his little sisters sadly that no one seemed to know where their father had disappeared to after their mother's funeral. He told them they were very lucky to all be together in this nice place.

Maggie came back out of her past when a very loud bang sounded out on the highway in front of the building. She looked out at the neglected lawn and fountain, thinking back to how it used to look. There had been watermelon-colored crepe myrtles touching one another around the circular driveway, blooming from spring until the first frost. The front lawn was always an emerald green and the spray of water from the fountain made everything look cool, even in the hundred-plus-degree Texas heat.

Her eyes moved over to the left, to the old red and white brick pergola that stood like a soldier guarding the formal garden. It was open on all sides to the breezes, and there was always a breeze on that high hill. There were little cement benches where one could sit and rest. What secrets it could tell: young love's first kiss, visions of floating ghosts on moonlit nights, and diaries scribbled in an uncertain hand. Maggie remembered that sometimes the ghosts floated in the dark halls of the girl's building. There would be a cold gust of wind and the lingering smell of a perfume, like the roses her mother loved so much. She wondered now if that was wishful thinking, as Sister never had the experience. If Brother did, he never would admit it. She looked wistful as she remembered. He did not like to talk of their past, and would quickly change the subject. Maggie realized as she got older, and Sister agreed, that it was just too painful for him to return to that part of his life.

Maggie walked down the stairs until she could see over to the shell of the building where the girls once lived. Lightning had struck the roof and caused a fire that left everything black, and the heat had burst all the windowpanes. She closed her eyes and could see it again as she saw it that first time . . .

Dr. Stanley, the superintendent, called over to the girls' cottage to tell Miss Haney that he was bringing over two sisters, ages six and nine. He let Brother give his sisters a hug and then one of the older boys was called to take him to his room in the Big Building. He promised his sisters that he would see them later that evening, and told them to be good. He felt guilty as he had promised his mother he would look after his sisters, but he would get permission to see them often. He never broke his promise as long as they were at the Home. Dr. Stanley carried their one small suitcase that contained what few belongings the girls had. Maggie grabbed his free hand and skipped backwards as they went across a smaller green lawn toward a two-story building. It had a porch with big white columns across the front. Maggie turned to grab Sister's hand and was given a reassuring squeeze in return. Maggie was too young to realize it at the time, but her sister became her mother that day.

A very large lady came to the front door, and Dr. Stanley introduced the girls to their new housemother, Miss Haney. She smiled at them, but it seemed to Maggie that the smile on her mouth did not reach her eyes. She took the one suitcase from Dr. Stanley and asked if that was all. Sister blushed, but Maggie was too busy looking around to notice. Dr. Stanley told Miss Haney that the girls could visit their brother at the pergola after supper. He had pointed it out to them on the way over. It was a little, open red and white brick structure in a pretty little garden between the two buildings.

Maggie hugged Dr. Stanley's legs as he said goodbye, and thought to herself: "Now I have me a daddy." Miss Haney told her later that she was not to hug Dr. Stanley. It was not nice.

Maggie ignored that instruction, and he became her "Pappy." She gave him lots of hugs over the years. He never seemed to mind.

The girls found out with great sadness that they could not be in the same room, as roommates were assigned according to age. They both had two roommates and were at opposite ends of the hall. When they went to meet Brother that evening after supper, which really tasted good, he told them that he had one roommate his age and thought he would like him just fine. He was to work at the dairy barn and help milk the cows as he had done that at his former home. He was relieved that both girls liked most of the food, and he said he would keep in close touch.

That first night Maggie did not sleep well without Sister, but her nice roommate, Lana, gave her a stuffed purple rabbit to sleep with. When Sister awoke, Maggie and the rabbit were at the foot of her bed.

All the rooms upstairs were similar, with little metal twin beds painted different colors. Each girl had a small closet and two drawers in a metal dresser. There was a large bath at each end of the hall with a shower and a tub. The toilet stalls had doors that latched, and there were four sinks with a mirror above each. Miss Haney had a large room at the front of the building with her own bath. Across the hall from her was the infirmary, or sick room, and bath. The building held twenty-five girls, and Maggie and Estelle were just lucky there was room for them the day they arrived.

Miss Haney was thrilled when she showed the girls the downstairs and found out that Sister could already sew and cook. She also was quiet and mannerly, and that was a plus for her. Maggie was excited when she saw the study-library, as she was just learning to read. She loved books. Sister read to her and helped her. She hoped she could continue. Reading was encouraged, and a contest was held in the summer. A prize was given for the one who read the most books. Maggie would win this the summer she was ten.

There was a big living room at the end of the hall with two sofas and lots of chairs. A fireplace with amber coals centered the room. Above the mantle was a portrait of a pretty lady who had big brown eyes and dark wavy hair. Maggie thought she looked like her mother. Down the hall from the library was a music room which held a small piano and several chairs. Hymns were played and sung there each morning, with one of the older girls playing the piano and another leading the singing. A devotion was also read after the hymns were sung. Maggie loved to sing, and sometimes sang the wrong words too loudly. Sister sang softly and sweetly. Brother led the singing at the boys' building in a very short time, as he had a wonderful tenor voice.

There was a full basement with a playroom at either end, a craft room, and two small bathrooms with a foot tub that was used in the summer when the girls went barefoot. All their feet were washed and dried before they could go upstairs. That way the sheets were kept clean for rest hour after lunch. Maggie made fast work of this exercise and was in and out of the foot tub before anyone else. She loved to be first in line for lunch and supper. The same foot washing was done in the evening in the summer also. The foot tub towels were something to behold by sundown each day. They went into the laundry almost immediately and were taken to the Big Building and washed by the older girls. Maggie did not ever want to become an older girl.

Maggie, Estelle, and Alex were called to the Big Building office the next day to tell Miss Clark goodbye, as she had spent the night there. She told them she would write, and that she was so glad to leave them in such good hands. They all hugged. True to her word, she and Brother wrote until he graduated, and he went back to Ralls to see her. She made all the difference in their lives.

Again Maggie was shaken out of her reverie by the arrival of several cars of laughing men and women, the Little Woodmen, as they called themselves. Maggie knew they all had a yarn to spin about their days at the Home. Those special times would be lost forever if she didn't get the stories written, or taped, or put on a floppy disc. She felt that she knew most of their stories, yet there might be a really good one she had missed.

Even if the old place couldn't be saved, at least there could be a collection of memories of simple pleasures, from a time that is no more. Maggie hurried to meet her friends.

Chapter 2
The Great Green Tree

The big boys are coming!
The big boys are coming!
Oh what a month this will be.
The big boys are coming!
The big boys are coming!
With the Great Green Tree!
Wheeeeeeeeeeeeeeee!

Christmas! The best possible time for kids at an orphan-age! The gifts! The secrets! The decorations! The smells! And best of all, the Christmas pageant!

The "big boys," which is what everyone called the boys at the Home who were sixteen and older, always went with the farm foreman to Oklahoma to get two Christmas trees. Actually, they were Mountain Cedars, one bigger than the other. The largest went to the Big Building and the smaller went to the Little Building. All the kids would anxiously wait

9

for the return of the flatbed truck and the two trees. They would be strapped down, but some of the boys would ride with the trees to make sure they stayed secure. It was an honor to be chosen; and Alex, Estelle and Maggie's big brother, was always one of the ones picked. He was in charge of some of the landscape projects at the Home and knew trees. They were always so proud to see him smiling as he held on to the biggest tree.

When the truck finally came back with the trees, they built heavy wooden stands and secured the largest tree in the dining room of the Big Building. It took all of the boys available to get the tree up the front steps and into the dining room. Then they would all jump on the back of the flatbed and ride over to the Little Building. There they would make a stand and take the smaller tree into the entry and then down the hall to the living room. The girls clapped and danced around the tree.

All the children who lived at the Home, usually twenty-five boys and twenty-five girls, decorated both of the trees. The retired members also were invited to help, but usually they just enjoyed watching. The craft room in the basement of the girls' building was full of red and green paper chains, red and white candy canes, and white angels made from lace doilies. It took the first week in December to get all of the decorations up. The big boys and big girls had to put on the lights of every color, and last the gold and silver tinsel was carefully draped. The superintendent and his wife directed these two last steps. The lights were not turned on until a special night when all gathered around the grand piano to sing Christmas anthems. The dining room lights would be turned off, and the giant Christmas tree's lights would be turned on with lots of "*oooooooohs* and *aaaaaaaaaaahs*." The retired members were like grandmothers and gave the children lots of attention and love. They also made quilts that were folded and put on the end of each girl's twin bed.

Packages would start to arrive just after Thanksgiving. Since at least one of the children's parents was deceased, each was assigned Another Mother, a Big Sister, and a Grove. These people all belonged the Woodmen Circle Fraternal Organiza-

Estelle in the kitchen at the Home.

Alex, third from left, with other "big boys."

tions, similar to the Eastern Star Lodge. There were only women who belonged to this fraternal group, as all the Woodmen Circle Board of Directors were women, state directors were women, salespersons were women, and they sold only to women. The year was 1929!

All the Christmas gifts had to be opened by the staff and listed by each child's name. Then they had to be rewrapped in Christmas paper, and tags put on. A careful check was done to make sure that everyone received the same number of gifts. The Home had a Christmas fund to buy toys and fruit and nuts to fill the stockings that each little girl and little boy hung at the foot of their bed. Even though the children and retired members had wonderful memories of Christmas, the staff had big headaches.

The national president, Mrs. Talbot, had no children of her own, but claimed all fifty of the children as hers. She always came at Christmas and brought everyone presents, including the retired members and the staff. She also remembered everyone's birthday. During World War II, she sent out a newsletter to all the boys and girls who were in the service or college, giving news of each and their current addresses. The boys especially enjoyed this, as sometimes it was all the news they got when they were overseas. She always came for Christmas, just in time for the Christmas Eve Pageant.

The pageant was the biggest thrill of the whole season. Everyone who wanted to could try out for the different parts. There were Mary, Joseph, the three Kings of the Orient, shepherds, and the Host of Heavenly Angels. Mary wore a lovely blue scarf that covered her head and shoulders, Joseph a striped tunic, the Shepherds wore burlap gowns and carried crooks, and the Angels were all in flowing white with crepe paper wings and halos made of wire circles covered with tinsel.

One particular Christmas, Estelle achieved her goal—to be Mary. Alex had a nice clear voice, and wearing a gold cloth robe he sang sweetly: "We Three Kings." At long last, Maggie got to be one of the Hosts of Angels. As she flew into the dining room, flapping her arms wildly, she knocked off her halo, much to her dismay. Under the halo she had worn her Indian beaded headband, complete with purple mountains and orange suns. There was soft laughter being choked down as she flew to pick up her halo. Needless to say, she never got to be Mary, as one had to be very well behaved; but one of her dolls did get to be Jesus in the manger one year. The entire chorus sang "Away in a Manger," very sweetly.

Special guests were always invited. First was the national president of the Woodmen Circle Insurance Company, Mrs. Talbot, and she brought gifts for everyone in her big black limousine. She had a driver who carried in all of the presents. He would stay and enjoy the night. All of the merchants in town who gave the Home discounts at the grocery and clothing stores came, as did the manager of the movie theater. All were given free passes to go to the movie once a week during school term, and they could go twice a week in the summer.

Teachers from town were invited to the Christmas program. At the country school there were only two; but after a new bus was given, the kids went into town to school, and there were a lot of teachers to invite. Most of them came, as it was a fun way to spend Christmas Eve. Everyone brought his or her family, as did the farm foreman. He had a sweet wife and six children, and they were accepted into the Home family. Santa never forgot them when he passed out presents.

As the program ended, the guests would leave, but all of the children and retired members would remain for the arrival of the Santa for the boys. The girls would then go home, put their pajamas on, and wait in the living room for Dr. Stanley to come over to read Charles Dickens' *A Christmas Carol*. He read with such feeling and all were as quiet as mice. Then he would leave, and with a jolly voice he would always say: "Merry Christmas to all, and to all a good night." He would be back the next morning to be Santa, and he didn't even have to wear a red suit. After he had breakfast with the girls, which was also special, he would go back to the main building. Maggie knew she would see him again at the dinner, as all gathered in the big dining room. Gifts were displayed on beds, with lists of who had given them. Thank-you notes were written on Christmas afternoon, before gifts were put away. Then the kids could play.

The girls wore their Sunday dresses to the Big Building

for dinner, as it was a very special occasion. All gathered for devotions around the grand piano, and Dr. Stanley would then play for them to sing Christmas anthems. Mr. Jim and his wife, the Home cooks, prepared a turkey dinner, complete with dressing, cranberry sauce, sweet and Irish potatoes, green beans, and pumpkin pie. All ate until they nearly popped. It was only then that the Great Green Tree began to lose its magic.

The decaying and vandalized buildings still stand west of town, high on that windy hill. It has been said that if one were to stand outside the broken dining room windows at Christmas time, the clear, sweet voices of little children might still be heard singing:

"Away in a manger, no room for his bed, the little Lord Jesus laid down His sweet head . . ."

CHAPTER 3
The Baptism

Maggie knew at age ten that she would love Mick O'Brian, age twelve, forever. He had two brothers, Tim and Sean, but Mick was the one who stole her heart one summer when he did a swan dive off the diving board at the lake. He was tall and thin, yet muscular, from throwing bales of hay onto the flatbed truck during harvest. But more than his physique were his green eyes and his long, black eyelashes that looked even longer when they were wet. He would put his arms out wide, make sure everyone was looking, then jump up and down on the board until he was high in the air, then go head first into the water with hardly a ripple. When he came up, everyone would clap and he would smile with his sparkling white teeth shining in his tanned, handsome face.

Tim and Sean were cute boys, but Mick had that certain something that made girls' hearts flutter from age ten to teens. All of the kids at the Home were encouraged to think of each other as brothers and sisters, but all knew better.

The O'Brian boys came to the Home when they were five, seven and nine, Mick being the middle boy. Their father was

15

gassed in World War I, and was in a veterans' hospital. Their mother had been a county clerk in Oklahoma, and from the one photograph the boys had, she was very beautiful. She had a life insurance policy that would provide a home for her boys in case of her death or disablement. She had died suddenly of complications of appendicitis, and the boys stayed with an aunt for a short time. It was during the depression, and the aunt did not have money to care for them. She drove them to the orphanage in North Texas, where they were put into the girls' building for a short time, until they adjusted to not having their mother. The housemother was especially good at caring for small children, both boys and girls. By the time that Maggie, her sister Estelle, and her brother Alex arrived at the Home, the O'Brians were at the boys' building.

Their mother had been a member of the First Christian Church in Oklahoma, so the boys went to that same church in town. Instead of once a month, as it was done in most churches, communion was served each Sunday at that church. The boys would see the crackers and grape juice passed each week, but as they had not been baptized, they could not partake. They would begrudgingly pass the trays on without having any. One Sunday, Mick whispered to both brothers when the minister asked anyone who wanted to profess their faith to come forward. All three boys went forward, and the minister spoke quietly to each one individually. As they answered, they shook their heads up and down. The minister then turned to the congregation and introduced the three brothers from the Woodmen Circle Home who had accepted Jesus as their Savior and who wanted to be baptized into the First Christian faith. He asked them some questions, to which they answered "yes." There was not a dry eye in the house. The official baptism would take place that night after the evening service.

Everyone had lunch at the Big Building after church on Sundays. Dr. Stanley would ask questions about the content of the sermon at each of the churches attended. He would call on different people each Sunday, so all the kids listened and wrote something down they remembered their minister saying. When he called on Mick to say a few words about the First Christian Church sermon, Mick was stumped, but recovered in

16

time to say that he and Tim and Sean were going to be baptized that night after the evening service. Dr. Stanley looked surprised, but Maggie just looked at Mick adoringly. It was then announced that anyone who wished to do so could go to the O'Brian boys' church to see them baptized. Maggie looked at her sister, and she nodded and smiled.

After lunch, as they walked back to their building, they came face to face with Mick. He smiled, more at Estelle than Maggie, but she didn't notice. She just smiled sweetly and said to him, "That's swell that you're gonna be baptized tonight. Sister and I are going to come to watch."

But sweet Estelle looked shyly at him and asked, "Did you have to go down to the front of the church and say that you believed in Jesus as your Savior?"

Mick smiled in his captivating way and Maggie barely heard his answer over the pounding of her heart.

"Yeah, he asked us all that stuff, and we said "yes," but what we really want to do is have grape juice and crackers every Sunday." He laughed as though he had just told a joke.

Estelle looked shocked, but Maggie didn't. She just looked. "See you tonight, Mick." She took off running, so he couldn't see her blush.

He shook his head and smiled at Estelle as he headed toward the garage where Dr. Stanley parked. He and some of the other boys went there to look for cigar butts that Dr. Stanley threw away. They would save them until they got to spend the night down at the log cabin by the lake, where they would light up and puff away. No one ever knew which of the boys were there the night the cabin burned to the ground, and no one ever told. All were punished by not seeing a movie for a month.

Several of the girls, boys, and retired members went on the bus to the First Christian Church to see the O'Brian boys baptized. Dr. Stanley took the three of them with him in his car, as they had to go early to get instructions about the baptism, and to get fitted in starched, white robes. Maggie, Estelle, and Alex were among those who rode the bus to town for the big event.

After the evening service, the minister disappeared

17

behind the pulpit and then, "Lo and Behold," a portion of the wood paneling slid to one side and there was a huge water tank, called a baptistery, that looked like a river. The minister had put on a long, white, starched robe, and surprisingly walked down some steps into the water. It came up to his waist. The O'Brian boys were supposed to come to the top step one at a time, but they had escaped their teacher, and all appeared at one time in their little white robes. As the minister held out his hand to the tallest boy, all three jumped in at once, making a great splash and soaking the minister. They swam under water, between the poor man's legs, and came up on their backs, spurting water like whales.

All of a sudden, Dr. Stanley stood up in the congregation, gave his famous two-sharp-blast-whistle, and the three boys came to attention. They went back to the steps, and mildly as you please, came one at a time to be baptized "in the name of the Father, the Son, and the Holy Ghost." There was considerable snickering among the kids from the Home, but Alex gave Estelle and Maggie a look that meant, "Don't even smile."

The assistant pastor dismissed people as the regular minister was too soaked to come back out. When everyone got on the bus to return home, the three O'Brian boys were missing. They rode back with Dr. Stanley, but no one ever knew what he told them on the way home. All Maggie knew was that she did not see her precious Mick, or his brothers, at a single movie for over a month.

All three of the boys bragged every Sunday about how much they enjoyed having crackers and grape juice each week. The other kids knew in their hearts that the O'Brian brothers had paid dearly for that little treat.

CHAPTER 4
The Longest Shower

The kids at the Home were reminded all the time that they were like brothers and sisters. They were to think of each other at least as friends, but never anything more. Most knew the difference.

One of the older girls, Diane, age fifteen, was already turning boys' heads, as she was so gorgeous. Her light brown hair fell in waves to her shoulders and her green eyes were made more dramatic by her dark, curling eyelashes. Sparkling white teeth would shine when she smiled—and she smiled a lot, especially at Wayne, age seventeen, who was so smitten by the love bug that he would turn all shades of red when she flashed one of those smiles at him. He even got bold enough to sit by her on the bus going to school and to church. He was a handsome boy in his own right. From all his harvesting of wheat in the summer, his shoulders and arms were muscular. Crystal blue eyes danced in his tanned face every time Diane would look at him, smiling. They were able to write secret messages to each other at school and press them into each other's trembling hands. A stolen kiss in the red and white gazebo went unnoticed, so they became more daring.

One fall night when the moon was full, final plans were made for them to meet. Wayne pretended to take a shower, locking the bathroom door behind him. The boys' rooms and baths were on ground level, so it was easy to go out the casement window. In the meantime, since it was 10:30 at night, the girls' building was dark. Diane slipped down the stairs and unlocked the front door for Wayne to enter. He went immediately to the living room just as they had planned. They wildly hugged and kissed and whispered words of young love, looking at each other in the moonlight.

Miss Haney had just dropped off to sleep when she thought she heard the front door click. She grabbed her flashlight that she kept by her bed and made her way to the staircase. As she got near the bottom, she heard soft murmuring and stopped to listen. She turned off the flashlight before she went toward the voices. She entered the living room and gasped at what her old-maid-eyes beheld! She told Diane and Wayne to straighten their clothes while she went to the interhouse telephone to call Dr. Stanley. He rushed over and told both of them that their next of kin would have to be called and that they would be packed and gone before morning. Wayne told Diane that since his mother lived in Fort Worth, he would take her with him until they could locate her brother, who was her guardian.

Before the sun came up, Diane and Wayne were packed and loaded into the poor mother's car bound for Fort Worth. Some of the girls in Diane's room were the only ones in that building who knew anything, and they just said she left in the night. The boys' bathroom door was unlocked, the shower turned off, and only the roommate who awoke knew what happened to Wayne. He was told not to talk. He never did.

Years later, the real story was told. Wayne wanted to marry Diane, but she was too young and had to go live with her unhappy brother. She later lived in California, and during WWII several of the boys from the Home who were stationed near her town went to see her. She was pretty enough to be a movie star, and got close to being one. She married a movie director and had several children. Wayne served in the navy in the war and later married. The ones from the Home who knew the true story bet that he never took a shower without thinking of his first love and the night the moon stood still, and the shower ran . . . and ran . . . and ran.

CHAPTER 5

The Parachute Jump

It was the middle of summer at the Home and all the little girls and boys had to rest from 1:00 until 3:00. Maggie was bored. She did not like to take naps and always found something under her bed to play with. She had tiny shells she had gathered from the park, a jar with holes in the lid with snails in it, or dead butterflies. She had strung all of the shells several days earlier. The snails had been fed with food she put in her pocket from lunch. She was still thinking of what to do with the pretty butterfly wings when a great idea came to her. She looked over at her two roommates, Lana and Jane.

"I have a great idea! Remember that show we saw at the beginning of the summer where the guy bailed out of the little plane and sailed down to earth with his parachute?"

"Yeah, I remember," they both said at the same time.

"So what?" asked Lana, rolling her eyes at Jane. "Is this another one of your made-up games?"

"This is the very best one I have ever thought up," said Maggie in her most excited voice. "This will really be fun!"

She jumped from her bed like a frog and tiptoed down the hall. In a few minutes she returned with an umbrella from the hall closet. She then looked in her dresser and took a leather belt that had belonged to her brother, Alex. Her eyes were sparkling with excitement as she told the girls to bring their pillows and come to the window.

"I am going to make you each a parachute, but Lana gets to go first." She took Lana's pillow and strapped it around her bottom with the leather belt. Handing the umbrella to Jane, she unlatched the screen of the window, and held it open, checking to make sure that the bushes were right below. Their bedroom was on the second floor, but the bushes would keep Lana off the ground.

"Now Jane, you hand her the umbrella for her to open as she gently jumps into the bushes below. It will act like a parachute and make her float." Jane looked worried and Lana looked scared. Maggie patted Lana on the back and told her it would be such fun. She promised each of them that they could wear her new ruby ring for a few days if they cooperated.

It took a bit of persuasion, but Lana jumped first, complete with pillow and umbrella. She landed, *kerplunk*, into the not-so-soft bushes. She looked up and angrily shouted: "I thought you said I would float!"

Maggie motioned her to be quiet and to come back up. She quickly told Jane that Lana just did not do it right and should have jumped up. Then the air would catch under the umbrella and make it float. Jane looked doubtful, but Maggie smiled and showed her the ruby ring again. As soon as Lana gave her the belt, Maggie got Jane ready to try her jump.

"Remember what I said about getting air under the umbrella. You'll just float like a feather." She held the screen open for Jane, and up—then down—she went.

Kerplunk. She, too, fell like a rock and not like a feather.

"I'm gonna tell Miss Haney on you, Maggie. You know she told you to quit making up games!" Maggie held up the ring and told her to hurry and come up. Both girls told her she had to jump, too, but Maggie told them she had to get a better umbrella and that she was now going to play "Nurse Nancy" and doctor their scratches. She slipped up the hall to get the bottle of "monkey blood" to doctor them with.

At that exact moment, Miss Haney decided to check the little pitter-patter of bare feet she heard in the hall. She had very good ears and heard every noise. Maggie was caught red-handed in the medicine kit. Miss Haney went to check out what the medicine was needed for, and found Lana and Jane sitting on the side of their beds covered with scratches. Then both girls told Miss Haney that Maggie made up this game of "parachute," and it was not fun at all.

That did it. Maggie was told she could not see a movie for the rest of the summer, and it was only the end of July. And because of the danger of the game, after rest hour she would have to go to the office and tell Dr. Stanley what she had done. That was the worse thing of all, because she was afraid he would not let her sit beside him anymore when he played and sang funny songs like "Watermelon, Watermelon, That's the Fruit for Me."

Miss Haney doctored Lana and Jane's scratches, and told all three girls to hush and get to sleep.

Maggie closed her eyes, wondering why, oh why couldn't she have just been happy with her shell necklace, or playing with her pet snails . . . *maybe, just maybe she could have a snail race and let Lana and Jane pick a winner . . . maybe bet a penny . . . she would write down a few rules and what the prize would be . . .* Maggie kept planning as her eyes closed, and she drifted off to sleep, smiling.

CHAPTER 6
Fireflies and Ghost Stories

Summertime! . . . No study hour . . . No early bedtime . . . Swimming. And the most favorite thing—catching fireflies and listening to Dr. Stanley tell ghost stories!

After supper, when all the kitchen chores were done, the girls would go outside to play badminton or *Piggy Wants a Signal*. Maggie was no good at badminton; she couldn't hit the little ball with feathers far enough to go over the net. Sister could. So Maggie usually played *Piggy,* as she was good at finding places to hide. It was like *Hide and Go Seek*, except that whoever was caught and put in the pigpen could get a signal from someone hiding. This had to be done skillfully, so the one giving the signal would not give away her hiding place. Only the girls played these games. The boys had their own games, such as football, baseball, and running races. They played on the front lawn of the Big Building. There were no joint games, but when the boys played football with boys from

Maggie's "Pappy," Dr. Stanley.

town on Saturdays, the girls got to watch. They liked that . . . a lot.

Dr. Stanley would sometimes come early and referee the badminton game until it became dark. He would give lessons on how to serve and return, and he would even play if he wanted to.

But the fun really began on the nights he decided to tell ghost stories. First he would show them lightning bugs, or fireflies as he called them, how to catch them and put them in glass jars. Three or four of the girls would share a jar, and then they would all gather on the front porch to listen to Dr. Stanley tell the very best ghost stories. All the girls gathered at his feet, as close as they could get. Maggie always managed to get the closest, as she would quit catching fireflies and slip up by his chair.

He would clear his voice, take a big puff of his cigar, blow out a cloud of smoke and begin: *"Once upon a time . . ."* He would make his voice scary at different times, then he might even lead up to a loud "BOO." No matter how many times he said it, everyone would scream and jump out of their skins. Then he would laugh and tell them it was time for bed. He would walk toward the Big Building with a lucky girl holding each of his hands. Maggie managed to get a hand more often than not. At the end of the sidewalk, he would turn and say "BOO" again, and everyone would scream and run into the building. Miss Haney would often shake her head and mumble, "Now I won't get them settled down for hours."

Sure enough, there would be whispering way into the night, and Maggie would be awake the longest. One night she felt a cold breath and the fragrance of rosewater and glycerin, her mother's favorite perfume, and she put her pillow over her head. She thought she felt someone tuck her sheet around her shoulders. She didn't tell Sister.

CHAPTER 7
Fright on the Basement Stairs

There were many ways the girls' housemother, Miss Haney, punished girls who broke her rules. She could spank, really hard, as she had a very big hand with about two hundred pounds behind it. She knew that spankings only made Maggie worse, and for a long time she found that keeping her home from the movies was her best bet. One hot summer day she was so angry with Maggie that she went beyond what was acceptable.

On that day one of the little girls came in the kitchen with her fine platinum hair half-curled and half-burned, crying, "Maggie did it. She said she could make my hair like hers, with curls, and she burned my head." Miss Haney knocked on the kitchen window and motioned for Maggie to come in. She asked her to explain why she was using the curling iron Miss Haney had thrown away.

"I found it in the barrel out back, and since it was in the hot coals, I pulled it out with a rake, so I could curl hair. Jane

28

wouldn't sit still and I only got to do one curl before she jumped up and hit the hot iron. A little of her hair was still in the curling iron, and SHE pulled it out, and not me! I told her I was sorry, but she wouldn't listen."

Miss Haney was red in the face from the steam in the kitchen where she and some of the big girls were canning peaches. She got redder, jerked Maggie by the arm, and shook her as she led her toward the dark basement steps:

"Go to the bottom step, and do not get up until I come for you." She gave her a shove, and Maggie stumbled down the steps, stopping her fast descent by putting her hand on the wall and bracing herself. Tears were running down her cheeks as she sat and looked into the gloomy hallway. There was a playroom at either end of the hall, but no light from their windows reached the step where she sat. The darkness seemed to wrap around her and almost choke her. There were eerie noises from the furnace room and unexplained shadows up and down the hall. She knew in her ten-year-old mind that these were the same steps she went down to go play in the playrooms on rainy or cold days, but there was always a light on the basement stairs. Now there was no light shining, as Miss Haney had made sure the light was off.

All of a sudden, Maggie thought she saw a shadowy figure float down the hall. She knew in her heart it was a ghost, and she put her head on her knees and realized she was trembling.

"Why am I always in trouble?" she said aloud, and even her own voice scared her. "I want to be good, but I seem to find ways of getting into trouble, no matter how hard I try to be good. Sister is never in trouble. Why can't I be more like her?" She wished with all her heart that Sister could come out of the kitchen and rescue her. Oh, how she wished this could happen!

All of a sudden she felt someone sit beside her, and put an arm around her shoulders to comfort her. She knew it had to be Sister, and she found herself getting very sleepy. When she finally awoke, the light was turned on, and Miss Haney's full figure filled the opening at the top of the stairs. Maggie reached to take Sister's hand, but no one was beside her. She

29

flew up the stairs and out the back door. When Sister finished canning, she came outside to see if Maggie was all right. Maggie thanked her for coming down and keeping her company on the dark basement steps.

"But honey, I could not leave the kitchen since Miss Haney was watching me. You must have just wished for me so hard it seemed as though I was there."

Maggie shook her head in disbelief. "But who could it have been? Someone sat beside me and hugged me around the shoulders and I fell asleep. I seem to remember the smell of roses right before I went to sleep."

Estelle, who remembered that their mother wore rosewater and glycerin lotion, smiled at Maggie and said, "You probably have a guardian angel who watches after you. Isn't that nice to know?"

Maggie looked puzzled for just a moment, then took off skipping and singing: "I'll find a grasshopper sooner than you, do-dah, do-dah . . . I'll find a grasshopper sooner than you, all the do-dah day."

Estelle watched her little sister chase grasshoppers, and smiled. She had a warm feeling about Maggie's guardian angel.

When Maggie confided in Dr. Stanley that she was having nightmares, he looked into the matter. When he discovered that she had become afraid of the dark, and why, he told Miss Haney that no one was to be punished on the dark basement stairs again. Maggie was also allowed to keep a light burning in the hall outside her bedroom. Even when she grew up, she always slept with a night light.

CHAPTER 8
The Red Dress

Maggie smiled as she scribbled in her beloved Five Year Diary, under the date of February 19, 1938: "Today Nancy asked Mick to go to the dance at the end of the year with me. Well ol' Diary he acceped [as she spelled]. I could dance for joy, Number one on the Hit Parade is *Jeepers Creepers*, number two is *Hurry Home* and then that glorious, lovely, scrumptous [as spelled] *Penny Seranade* yum . . . yum."

It was wintertime, but Maggie thought as she closed her diary that all of the girls who were going to the dance would have to start thinking about their long dresses. She had never had a long dress, and she knew just what she wanted—a red dress, with puffed sleeves, a square neck, and full skirt with a ruffle around the bottom. She also wanted little black velvet bows on the sleeves, at the two corners of the neck and ever so often around the ruffle. She closed her eyes and could see Mick and herself dancing. Some of the boys had come over to a fish dinner and to practice dancing. She wrote in her diary that night: "Had fish supper, then danced tonight. Mick has improved his dancing

Left:
The Red Dress.
Below:
Maggie on the far left,
Estelle second from the
right, and friends.

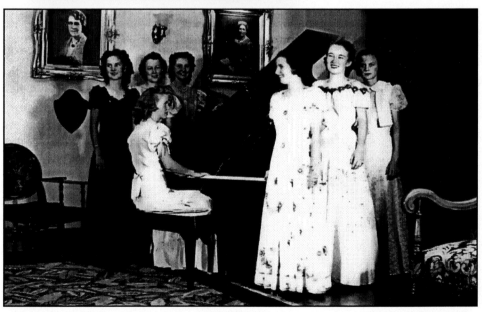

so much. I think he is just cute. Since he has been sick, I thought all the dancing would hurt him, but a few days later he went to the Doctor and he was better. I'm so glad. We can hardly wait for the dance in June. He got to sit at my table."

Dr. Stanley decided to let some of the big girls go into town with Miss Haney and pick out a long dress and shoes at the Dry Goods Store that gave the kids at the Home a discount. Sister came home after the first trip. She had found a pretty white taffeta dress with deep pink roses trimming the ruffle that dropped over her pretty shoulders. By the time that Maggie got to go, most of the dresses were picked over, and there was no red taffeta with black velvet bows. All the girls tried to tell her that the dance was in the spring and that a pastel dress would be much better. She begged Dr. Stanley, however, and since Miss Haney and the big girls would be making some of the dresses, he said she could buy red taffeta material and a pattern.

Maggie looked through the big pattern books in the material department and finally found the pattern for her dream dress. The cutting and the sewing of the remaining dresses took place in February, March, and April. Maggie was so excited when she tried on her dress. It was a little loose in the waist, but otherwise it was just like she had dreamed it would be.

June finally came. The dance was at the Municipal Building Ballroom, and there was a banquet first. This dance was to honor the High School Band and Orchestra, and little gold pins were given to all the members of these organizations. Maggie soon realized that most of the dresses were in pastel—spring colors—but she still loved her red dress with the black velvet bows. All the kids from the Home went on the bus and Mick sat by her, but he didn't have much to say. As soon as the dance began, one of his good friends from town, a boy who played the trumpet, cut in on them, and Mick immediately found a girl from town he had been seeing at school. They danced nearly every dance, and Maggie's heart broke very quietly. She smiled too much and pretended to be having a good time.

That night, when she hung up the red dress, never to be

put on again, she reached under her pillow and wrote in her diary: "Dear Diary, Tonight was the big event I've been talking about. I loved the banquet and everyone in the band and orchestra got a pretty gold pin. I was disappointed in the dance. I don't like *anyone* anymore like I used to." With those sad words written, she hung the red dress in the infirmary closet. Only later, when she had measles and was confined to that room, did she take out the red dress.

She took it out on the little black wrought-iron balcony and waved it to get King Arthur, the Home's big, bad bull, to snort and stomp his feet and bellow. She pretended she was a famous bullfighter and her beautiful red dress became her magic cape. She would swish it to the right and yell, "OLE!" Then to the left, and a louder "OLE!" This was a lot more fun than dancing at that silly old dance. Maggie thought: *Someday I'll be a famous bullfighter, with a magic red taffeta cape with little black velvet bows! Then Mick O'Brian will be sorry!* Again she shook the red dress over the balcony and shouted, "OLE!"

CHAPTER 9
Dating Dilemma

While Maggie was having her dance problems in her red taffeta dress with the black velvet bows, her sister, Estelle, was having an adventure of her own, but not an unpleasant one. It seems that the young man who played the piano in the orchestra engaged for the dance spotted Sister in her white dress, with roses around the drop-shoulders, and liked what he saw. Somehow he managed to meet her during intermission and asked her for a date on the coming Sunday afternoon. He was staying at a mutual friend's sister's home and wanted to know if she could meet him there on Sunday afternoon before he had to leave town. He was without a car, nor did his friend have a car to pick her up. He gave her the address and telephone number so she could call him. He was already in college in another town, so he was older. The boy he was staying with was a junior in Sister's high school, and she knew him because he was in the band.

When she got up her nerve on Saturday, she told Miss Haney that she had met a boy at the dance who was in town for just the weekend. He had asked her to meet him at James

Stone's sister's home on Sunday afternoon for dessert and tea. Miss Haney had to talk it over with Dr. Stanley, who thought it would be all right if Maggie went also. He was sure the lady would not mind one extra person for dessert. It did not please Estelle at all that Maggie had to tag along, but when she called her new friend, Henry, he said that Maggie could be James' date. Maggie only agreed because her sister was always so good to her, and she felt she should help her out. Miss Haney was going into town to visit one of her sisters, and told Dr. Stanley she could take them and pick them up in a couple of hours.

Estelle was ecstatic. Maggie was not, as she knew this James boy in the band, and he was a bit on the wild side. But she kept her mouth shut so as not to ruin Sister's excitement.

When they arrived at the home of James' married sister, James ran out to the car and told Miss Haney that his sister would come and meet her, but that she had run to the store for ice cream. It was agreed that 4:00 would be a good time for Miss Haney to come back to pick up the girls. She was partial to Estelle and wanted her to have a nice visit.

When the girls went into the house, there was soft music playing and the draperies were closed. Henry came to take Estelle's hand and disappeared to where the music was playing. James took Maggie's hand to lead her to a sofa.

"I'd like to meet your sister, James," Maggie said as she shook her hand loose.

"She'll be back in a little while, but in the meantime, you and I can get to know each other better. I sure thought you looked pretty in that red dress. I was sorry not to dance with you, but I had to help out and play guitar in Henry's orchestra."

Maggie was not sure what to do next, but decided to get the Sunday paper and look at the comic strip. She sat on the floor, however, and not the sofa. James seemed to think that was a good idea and sat down very close to her and started to touch her hair, and then her face. She jumped up to run and find her sister.

"Sister, where are you?" she called out in a loud and nervous voice. She ran to the room where the music was coming from, and there was her sweet, shy big sister in an embrace like one in the movies!

36

"Hi, Sweetie," Estelle's face turned blood-red and the young man turned to James and angrily said, "Keep her occupied! Can't you see we are busy . . ah . . dancing?"

James took Maggie by the hand and practically dragged her out of the room and back to the living room. He grinned as he said, "Don't be such a spoil-sport, kid. My sister went to the show, and won't be home for a couple of hours, so we have all that time to get . . . acquainted." He pulled her toward him, but she made a dash for a small chair across the room. She knew in her heart it was going to be a long afternoon—and a dangerous one for she and Sister both.

Just as James approached her again, the telephone rang and he had to go answer it. "Hey, Henry! Break it up back there. The lady is on her way to pick them up as she has an emergency to take care of. They are to be out front in ten minutes." Maggie was already grabbing her purse and heading for the door. She was never so glad to get out of a house in her life, and she hoped that Sister had learned her lesson, too!

Estelle lingered just inside the door as she and Henry whispered their good-byes. As Miss Haney drove up, Maggie jumped in the front so Sister could wave goodbye to Henry.

"Well, did you girls have a good time? How was dessert?" Maggie chattered about how good the pie and ice cream was, how nice James' sister was, and what was Miss Haney's emergency? She told them that one of the little girls had fallen and she needed to go and make sure she was all right.

When they got home, Maggie ran ahead to kiss the child who had been hurt, and who had probably saved hers and Sister's lives. Then she ran back to confront her sister, with her hands on her hips and her brown eyes blazing.

"Don't ever take me on one of your dates again, especially with someone as fast as that James! You and Henry sure did hit it off in a hurry! You just left me stranded in another room with that octopus. I had to fight for my life! He was so . . . I don't know the right word . . . *creepy* . . . that's it!"

Estelle was still in a dream world with a silly grin on her face. "What did you say, honey? . . . He's going to write me from college, and at the end of summer he plans to come back. And then when I graduate and move to Omaha, Nebraska, he

37

is going to come visit me there . . . and . . . " humming to herself, she actually ignored her angry little sister, for the very first time in her life.

Maggie just shook her head in disbelief, stomped angrily up the steps, and sat on the porch. She thought to herself: *Boys! Deliver me! I would lots rather chase butterflies and grasshoppers! I think I'll go change clothes and do just that!* She jumped up, forgot about being angry, and flew into the house, leaving Sister talking and smiling to herself.

CHAPTER 10
Wild Violets, Lilacs, and Roses

Maggie loved flowers. All the girls were given a different duty each month, and she was always so happy when she was given the duty of working outside. Pushing the lawn mower was not fun, but it was better than pushing a big, heavy, smelly mop. The stuff that was poured in the water had the lingering odor of a hospital.

When Dr. Stanley finally planned a rose garden on the east side of the girls' building, Maggie got to help. There were weeds waist high to be cut down with a weed chopper. That was even fun, as she could pretend that she was a sword fighter, just like in the movies of knights or even pirates. The boys would then have to come with a plow like they used in the fields and dig up the roots of mainly Johnson grass. The garden plot was then raked by some of the big girls who wore big straw hats to protect their skin. Sister did not like the sun since it made her have more freckles, but Maggie never wore a hat. She just turned brown. The other little girls would gather the roots of the weeds in boxes to be loaded into the back of the Home's pickup truck and taken to be burned.

When it was time to plant the rose bushes, Dr. Stanley came to help. All colors were planted: red, yellow, pink, white, and a pinky-yellow called Talisman. That was Maggie's favorite. She did not like the white rose. It reminded her too much of Mother's Day when she, Sister, and Brother had to wear a white rose pinned to their shirt, blouse, or dress. Only the few kids who still had mothers could wear a red rose. Oh how Maggie wanted to wear a red rose!

On May 14, she wrote in her treasured diary: "Dearest Diary. Today is Mother's Day. I'm very thankful that I had my mummy as long as I did. I only wish that she was with me now."

When they all went to church, they would receive little smiles and pats as they went into their Sunday school class. Maggie often wished that they did not have to wear a rose at all. Then no one would feel sorry for them. She knew the nice town people meant well, but it always made her sad, and sometimes Sister would have tears in her eyes. Brother would just look more serious, and Maggie could see his jaw tighten.

She loved to hoe around the rose bushes and to give them a good soaking in the evening. Sometimes the hose would get away from her and she would spray water on someone, accidentally—especially anyone who had tattled on her during the week.

Lilacs were part of the original planned landscape and were banked at both the entrance and exit gates. Maggie could close her eyes and experience their fragrance. There were also many pink, white, and watermelon-colored crepe myrtle lining the circular driveway in front of the Big Building, but lilac was still her favorite fragrance.

On Mother's Day, the girls were allowed to gather wild-flowers for the retired ladies and take the bouquets to their rooms. Among these wildflowers were wine cups, wild foxglove, and Maggie's very favorite, the tiny wild violet. She knew all the secret places to go look, and she would take only Lana with her. "See Lana," she would explain as she squatted and brushed away decayed leaves. "You have to look really hard for the little

40

green, heart-shaped leaves peeking through. Then, after you take away the leaves of winter, there the violets will be."

"How did you ever find them?" Lana would say as she stooped to see the tiny flowers more closely.

"Well, you just have to use your eyes and go away from where we all run and play." She gathered several of the dark green leaves and put some of the pale orchid violets in the middle of the leaves. "We'll get Miss Haney to give us some little white paper doilies and we'll cut out the middle, like Sister has taught me, and stick the leaves and violets through the hole. Then we can tie a ribbon around the stems for our two favorite older ladies." All had their favorites who acted like grandmothers, and who stitched quilts for their beds. Only Maggie and Lana made the wild violet nosegays, as they kept the violets' whereabouts a secret.

On Mother's Day, a large vase filled with lilacs, roses, and crepe myrtle was put on the grand piano, and two of the older ladies carried small nosegays of wild violets. They always smiled sweetly at Lana and Maggie. This took away some of the sadness of having to wear the white rose each Mother's Day. When Maggie grew up, neither she nor Sister ever bought or planted white roses.

CHAPTER 11
"The Lonesome Cowboy"

Summer nights were long and boring for the boys. They worked hard all day harvesting the hay for the livestock to have food in the winter. The dairy had to be kept spotless, as the milk was a vital part of the diet of the children and the retired members, plus the staff. Gardens had to be kept planted to supply the vegetables for all year round, as very few canned goods were bought. Peach trees had to be pruned and sprayed to supply fruit for canning and for eating. Therefore, the boys were usually tired by the time they came in for the evening meal. Sometimes they played baseball or football, but in the summer they needed something special.

Maggie's brother, Alex, had a wonderful idea one summer when he was fifteen. He sang very well and could write a convincing story, as his A's in English would prove. He spent several nights after he finished his chores perfecting his drama, to be given on a Saturday night in July. It was to feature him singing "The Streets of Laredo," and he would perform in a play about a cowboy, which he had written. He would sing to a beautiful Mexican girl, who would be off stage, as none of

42

the older girls wanted to be in his drama. Maggie volunteered, but he said she was too young. Besides, he did not want to be upstaged by his little sister. Estelle said she would be Rosa, but he said she was too pale and her eyes were the wrong color. For once, she did not become sad, but smiled with relief.

Most of the kids had a little money from birthdays or Christmas. Each of the children at the Home had an Other Mother and a Big Sister who sent presents or money. Most of the time the money was put in an account in the child's name in the office, but sometimes they were given a few nickels or pennies to put in their pockets for something at school. Alex hoped to get paid for his performance, and he wrote on the poster: *A NIGHT WITH ALEX, THE LONESOME COWBOY . . . ADMISSION . . . 1 to 5 Cents*. He asked his good friend, Mick O'Brian, whom he called "Jarvis," to be at the door of the laundry room where the play was to take place, to take up money and give out tickets. Mick agreed, knowing he could pull a "good one" on his self-centered friend. He had to admit Alex was good-looking, with his black, shiny, wavy hair, brown eyes, and olive skin. He was also fairly tall, thin, and very neat in his appearance. Mick knew that he was next in line for Alex's clothes, and that Alex could give him help on homework. So he agreed to sell tickets for him.

The night of the play came, and the girls were also invited to come to the laundry room of the Big Building, and bring a contribution for admission.

The casement windows of the basement room had been opened wide, and all the lightbulbs but one had been twisted to off. Alex had row after row of metal chairs lined up like a theater, and he had even constructed a small stage out of scrap lumber that rested on cement blocks. He called Miss Haney on the house phone and told her the girls could come over but she should remind them to be quiet during his performance. He had a little more trouble getting the boys rounded up, and according to Mick's plan, it was just after sundown when all settled down. He held a tin cup for the admission fares and gave each kid a ticket in exchange. Alex had gotten Estelle to print the tickets and cut them out. Maggie was allowed to help her, a little.

All of a sudden, from behind a sheet curtain, Alex appeared with a guitar he had borrowed from the High School Band (he played the trumpet in the band). He strummed the guitar mightily, dressed in work pants, white shirt, wide-brimmed straw hat (no one had a cowboy hat to fit him), and a silk striped sash which Miss Haney had made for him. He also had the same striped material tucked into the neck of his shirt. He looked very dashing and handsome. Maggie started to clap, but Sister quieted her.

When Alex started to sing, his voice was sweet and clear . . . "As I rode down the streets of Laredo . . ." All was quiet. But as he continued, coyote howls came from different parts of the room. Alex kept right on with his serenade to the lovely Rosa, who remained off stage. As the play ended, there was supposed to be a storm, with Alex doing his own thunder on the guitar. As he started strumming the bass strings, Mick and some of the big boys, who had slipped outside, started spraying the Lonesome Cowboy with water from the garden hose. He ran from the stage, jumped through one of the windows, and a fight commenced outside the laundry room windows. The entire audience departed at one time, yelling and laughing and screaming.

Maggie and Estelle stayed to help their big brother clean up the mess and to tell him how good he was at singing. He finally found the tin cup and anxiously looked inside to see how much money he had made. Much to the dismay of all three, he had collected only 20 rocks, 15 shells, 10 beads, and a dead cricket. He was so mad, he went over to the window and emptied the cup.

After all the water in the room had been mopped up, the sheets folded, and the lumber and cement blocks stacked, he hugged both of his sisters and grinned:

"Well, girls, this was my big night. All the grown-ups liked my singing, and those boys are all just jealous, because all they can do is plow a field. You just wait, someday your big brother will be famous, and then they will all be sorry!" They both hugged him and agreed. He was their star, no matter what the other kids thought!

CHAPTER 12
The Barbed Wire Fence

It was a great adventure to get to go into town to school. Alex and the older kids had to be driven to the high school. The country school that was attended by the rest only went through the eighth grade. The ninth, tenth, and eleventh went to high school in town.

Either Dr. Stanley or Miss Haney would drive the older kids in a big car that was used by the staff for school or emergencies. Everyone else walked the two and one-half miles each day to the Blackbridge Country school no matter what the weather was.

Maggie was thinking about that school one day at rest time. She really missed the two teachers who taught them all for several years. Miss Nell taught grades one through four in one room, and Mrs. King taught grades five through eight in the other room. The school building was white frame with a porch across the front. There were twenty desks and a huge wood-burning stove in each room.

45

Maggie recalled that because she could read well, she skipped third grade and went on to fourth. This caused her to be in the same grade with some of the older boys. She loved to compete with them on the playground that was totally fenced by barbed wire.

One day she discovered several of the boys in her class were jumping over the fence, starting with a one-foot jump and ending with a three-foot jump. She thought that it looked easy enough and asked if she could join in. She was assured that she was too short to clear the barbs that stuck up every six to eight inches. Maggie promised that she would share her lunch with them if they let her jump. If she made the same jumps that they did, they would have to give her their apples as a prize.

All the other kids gathered around, cheering her on, but Estelle kept trying to get her to give it up. At the two-foot-high spot on the fence, all the boys but one went flying over the dangerous barbed wire. His long pants caught on one of the barbs and flipped him backwards. It scared him more than it hurt him.

Then it was Maggie's turn. Everyone was cheering her on, so she turned and bowed before she made the running jump. Her right leg made it just fine, but her left leg was not so lucky. She felt a sharp sting as the barb tore into her leg and held her fast. Estelle ran to get Miss Nell.

In the meantime, Lana and Jane got under her arms to hold her steady. Estelle and Miss Nell lifted her until the barb let go. Blood began to spurt as a blood vessel was hit. Tim O'Brian whipped out a clean, white handkerchief and folded it to a square. Then he told Estelle to sit Maggie down on the grass and apply pressure until the bleeding stopped. Most of the boys at the Home were in the Boy Scouts and knew what to do in emergencies. Tim got a badge for bravery at the next scout meeting.

There were no telephones at the school, so Miss Nell and Mrs. King decided that Estelle could help Maggie hobble the two and one-half miles back to the Home. First she had to sit very still until the bleeding stopped. A first aid kit at the school made it possible for Miss Nell to pour Merthiolate into the wound. A gauze bandage was wrapped around the injury, held in place by wide adhesive tape. Maggie was enjoying all the attention and thought the bandage was "keen." She did realize, however, that Miss Haney would be upset. All the children, in their little white uniforms, with green and purple capes, were to have their picture taken on the new engine of a Katy Railway advertisement. She was sure she could hide her leg with the big white bandage by standing behind someone. She mentioned this to Sister as they started the long walk home and said not to worry about that as she could stand behind her.

As they walked, Maggie would hop on one leg and hold on to Estelle to keep from falling. If she walked normally, her leg would throb. Just as they were getting close to the Dunbars' farmhouse, a car of men slowed down and asked if they wanted a ride. Sister started pulling Maggie toward the Dunbars' driveway and told them: "Thank you, but we live right here." Up the drive they went, and sure enough, Mr. Dunbar came out of the house and asked if they needed help. Maggie told him about her accident and that they lived at the Home just on top of the hill. He immediately called to his wife that he was taking the girls up the hill to the Home. Maggie and Estelle knew they were the luckiest two girls in the world.

Although the leg wound should have had stitches, Miss Haney just washed it good and poured more Merthiolate into the now swollen leg and rewrapped it. She shook her head when Estelle told her how it happened.

"Maggie, you just do too many dangerous things! You are not a boy, so why do you want to act like one? Your sister never gets hurt and you should just try to be more like her! I'm not sure Dr. Stanley will even want you in the Katy Railroad picture this Saturday. We'll just have to see."

When Dr. Stanley was called on the house phone, he came right over to the girls' building to see Maggie's injury. He wanted to take her to the doctor in town, but Miss Haney assured him that she had cleaned it again and doctored it. When she asked him about the pictures on Saturday, he hugged Maggie around the shoulder and said, "Of course she can be in the picture. No one will look at her leg; they'll be looking at her big smile."

And sure enough, when the picture was printed on the cover of the Katy Railroad magazine that summer, Maggie was right on the front of the engine with her white bandaged leg, smiling up a storm. All of the kids and some of the staff got free passes that June to the Insurance Convention in Joplin, Missouri, courtesy of the Katy Railroad.

But Maggie had learned her lesson. No more jumping with the boys across a barbed wire fence. However, when she was fourteen, King Arthur, the Big Bad Bull, chased her over another barbed wire fence. She felt sure he remembered her from the balcony, waving the red taffeta dress like a cape.

When she grew up, she was often reminded of her adventures with barbed wire fences. Her left leg bears a deep scar from jumping the one at school, or not jumping it. Her right leg has three long scars from climbing the fence to get away from King Arthur.

Maybe Miss Haney was right after all. She was a tomboy who loved challenges, and had the scars to prove it.

CHAPTER 13

Summertime

School was out for the summer! Shoes and socks were shed! The sun was shining! All was right with the world, and there were things to think of besides lessons and chores.

There were gardens to be planted, a week at Camp Grayson with the Camp Fire Girls, and the very best thing . . . swimming at the lake. Maggie felt for sure that this summer she would pass all the tests in the "pigpen" to graduate to the deep water. She laughed to herself as she thought of the shallow part that was fenced in, and fondly named the "pigpen."

Dr. Stanley knew when he first saw the lovely lake on the property that work would have to be done to make it safe enough for all the children. A bridge had been built across the far end where one could stand and fish. It also had a small log cabin where a boat was kept for emergencies, and some camping equipment. But the very best thing ever built, according to the little kids, was the beloved "pigpen." Dr. Stout had Mr. Camp, the farm manager who lived up the hill, and the older boys build a very large pen with a hardwood floor with a black wrought-iron fence around it. When the lake was very low, they sank four steel poles deep into the bottom of the lake, near the bank. These were anchored in cement. When the cement had set solid, they carried and attached the pen to the steel poles with metal clamps. This was a real engineering feat, but when the lake filled back up in the spring, the water level came to below the top of the wrought-iron fence. All the little kids who could not swim in the big lake could have fun in the pigpen. The older children who had been going to Scout Camp and Camp Fire Girls Camp could already swim. They could either go off the diving board into the lake or jump in from the bank.

Maggie always looked forward to watching Mick O'Brian do a perfect swan dive off the board. All of the girls would clap for him and the rest of the boys would be a little intimidated when it came their turn. As a result, most of the boys would do a cannon ball or a crazy dive and splash everyone in the pigpen. Maggie was sure that Mick was the best diver in the whole world. He was her hero, for sure.

When Maggie had passed all the tests to go into the deep water, Dr. Stanley whistled for Paul, Alex's best friend, to take charge of Maggie's first attempt at swimming in the deep water. Of course, Alex and Estelle had their eyes on them every minute. Alex was not as strong a swimmer as Paul, but he stood by just the same. As Maggie climbed over the wrought-iron fence, she glanced up at Dr. Stanley. He smiled and said to her, "You will be just fine, Maggie. You are a very good swimmer. Just don't get to going too fast and wear yourself out."

That was all she needed to get her confidence back, and off she went. It felt funny with no floor and just water under her, but it felt good and she just kept going. Paul thought they had gone far enough and called out: "OK, now let's turn around and go back."

Maggie had never turned around, and was not sure at all how to do that. She began to panic and thrash the water. Before Dr. Stanley could throw out the lifeline, she had grabbed Paul around his neck in a death grip and down they went. Paul swam under water until he saw one of the poles that held the pigpen. He was able to grab hold of it and pulled them both to the surface of the water with Maggie wild-eyed, spitting and coughing. She grabbed the side of the rail and held on for dear life. Then she looked up at Paul, who still had his arm around her waist, and through tears, voice quivering, she told him: "That was fun! But I need some practice on turning around, don't I?" He had no breath left to answer, but nodded his head up and down.

Dr. Stanley told her to come up the ladder and he rubbed her briskly with a big towel, gave her a hug, and quietly said to just her: "You swam just fine, honey, but we need to work on that turn. Take this towel and go over on the grass and lie down awhile. You had quite an adventure, didn't you?" Maggie just looked up and smiled and gave him a very wet hug around his waist.

She knew it would not be long before Big Jim and his wife would bring down the cold chicken, pimiento sandwiches, and cold watermelon in the back of the pickup truck. There would also be a great big milking container full of a red drink they all called "Pollypop." She was already feeling much better. She loved watermelon and had to smile to herself as she sang the little song Dr. Stanley played on the piano:

> "Watermelon, watermelon, that's the fruit for me,
> Jolly as can be, charming after tea.
> You can talk about peaches, pears, plums all three,
> But watermelon, watermelon, that's the fruit for me."

He always rolled his eyes at her when he sang. She did, too. It was such fun to laugh and sing with him. He could play anything on the piano and all the girls would join in. Maggie did not always get to sit on the piano bench beside him, but she was glad when she was lucky enough to get to.

Dr. Stanley went to her Methodist church, and she would always race to grab his hand and sit next to him. She would get Sister to sit on the other side of him and Brother would take turns sitting by his sisters. That was a warm and special thing. They all sang the hymns together. Dr. Stanley sang low, Brother a sweet tenor, Sister alto, and Maggie, just loud. They knew most of the hymns by heart and did not even have to look at the book, most of the time. Dr. Stanley would open his Bible to the Scriptures and let them follow along with him. Sometimes when

51

Maggie, ten years old.

the regular minister was sick or on vacation, Dr. Stanley would preach. That made all of them so proud, and they got to brag to all the other kids on the bus. He may not have been their birth father, but he was like a real father to Alex, Estelle, and Maggie.

The summer that Maggie turned ten, she got to go to the Camp Fire Girls' Camp at Camp Grayson. She was the youngest one there that summer, as her birthday was not until the end of July. She was allowed to go, even though one was supposed to already be ten in June when camp started. Two older girls served as camp counselors, the same sisters who came from town once a month during the year to teach them crafts and skills that would make them good Camp Fire Girls. That summer was really special as they had all either made, or had someone make, ceremonial gowns. These were to look like Indian leather dresses, but were made of tan heavy cloth with rickrack trim around the neck. The bottom of the dress and the edges of the sleeves were cut to resemble fringe.

There were many different colored beads to be earned by passing different tasks. These were for cooking, cleaning, camping skills, beading, etc. These beads were then strung on a long piece of leather and worn like a necklace. Maggie's favorite bead she wanted to earn was a big orange one that was given after a headband was carefully designed on graph paper, then beaded successfully. The project was started at camp but had to be finished at home.

There were cookouts where another bead was earned for preparing a dish on an open fire. Building the fire was another task to earn a bead. Maggie's favorite dish was "Smores." She took two graham crackers, put a square of chocolate bar on one, roasted a marshmallow on a green stick until it was squashy, put it on the other cracker, and smashed it all together. The hot marshmallow would melt the chocolate, and *yum*, a perfect dessert. The reason it was called "Smores" was that when you ate one, you always wanted "some more." Sister could do a whole meal in a piece of foil: vegetables, meat, everything, and it was really good.

Then there were swimming lessons. Maggie finally earned a bead for learning to swim and turn around. She could hardly wait to show "Pappy" and Paul.

53

With no chores or homework to do, and fun things going on every day, Maggie hated to think about camp coming to an end. What a wonderful time they all had! But there was always next year to look forward to, and beads to be earned all during the year. She intended to have a longer necklace than anyone, even Estelle.

When they returned home by bus, Dr. Stanley was there to meet them and to hear some of their experiences. He walked over to the big front porch, where he sat and listened to all their adventures. He was especially pleased that Maggie had learned to swim, and best of all, to turn around. All were given a chance to tell their favorite thing, and sometimes they all talked at once. Miss Haney, who had been on her vacation, sat and listened also. She was especially pleased about the girls who learned to cook, and planned to let them try their hand with regular cooking. All trooped upstairs to take a bath and put all their dirty clothes down the laundry chute to be washed the next day. All were ready to go to bed a little early, as they had had a busy week.

As Maggie's eyes got heavy, she was thinking to herself: *Now all I have to do to finish my headband is to make the mountains out of purple beads, the sun out of yellow beads, and the river . . . out . . . of . . .* and she smiled as she slept, and held her half-finished headband.

CHAPTER 14

Maggie's Secret

The national board of the insurance company that sponsored the Home was completely made up of women from all over the United States. The president, Mrs. Talbot, was originally from Texas, but had moved to Omaha, Nebraska, where the home office was located. One of the vice-presidents, Miss Mallory, was from Oklahoma, and another, Mrs. LaRue, from Pennsylvania. Maggie remembered these three in particular, as they had dinner with the girls at one of their meetings, held at the Home.

Miss Haney had been a nervous wreck, expecting everything to be perfect, for the dinner that she and some of the older girls were cooking. The outside of the building had to be perfect and Maggie was among the girls assigned to that duty. Maggie knew she would not be allowed in the kitchen, and loved working in the yard.

Estelle was of course asked to help with the dinner, which had to have special food, because the president was diabetic. There was to be a special fruit plate at her table, and the girls who were to sit with her were told not to eat the fruit but to eat the dessert served to them. Maggie and Estelle had been assigned to that table, but Maggie really wanted to sit at the table with Mrs. LaRue, as she was very pretty, like she remembered her mother, with big brown eyes, dark hair, and the sweetest smile. Her portrait was aboove the mantle in the living room.

Everything was spic and span, including the girls, when the ladies arrived for dinner. They had on the most beautiful dresses Maggie had ever seen. Mrs. Talbot's was a blue lace with a diamond pin at the neck. Miss Mallory had on a deep red silk, and she wore pearl earrings and a string of pearls. But Maggie could not keep from staring at Mrs. LaRue, who wore a soft gold floating dress. She found out later that the material was called chiffon. It was beaded with gold and brown shiny beads that caught the light when she walked and looked like twinkling stars.

Dinner was going along splendidly; all the dishes were perfect. There was baked chicken, rice, fresh green beans, banana pudding for dessert, and of course, Miss Haney's special yeast rolls that were light and fluffy. Maggie forgot, and when Mrs. Talbot asked if anyone wanted any of her fruit plate, her eyes lit up as she saw juicy slices of watermelon, surrounded by strawberries and grapes. Just as she opened her mouth to say "Yes ma'am," her sister gave her a swift kick on her ankle. She quickly recovered with a smile and replied, "No thank you." After the president had taken all the fresh fruit she wanted, she insisted that all of the girls have a piece also. Maggie got her watermelon after all and smiled sweetly at Mrs. Talbot. Estelle took a strawberry and smiled her thanks, too.

After dinner, everyone was walking to the living room from the dining room. Maggie kept very close to Mrs. LaRue, who finally looked down with her lovely smile and asked Maggie if she wanted to talk to her.

"Oh yes, ma'am, I have just been looking at your sparkling beads all night, and I was wondering . . ." she hesitated, and looked around to see where her sister was, not wanting another warning kick. "When you get through wearing that dress, could I please have it?"

Mrs. LaRue had to work hard to keep from laughing at

her sincere little face. "I'm afraid this dress would be way too big for you for a long, long time."

Maggie giggled and put her hand over her mouth. "I didn't mean for me to wear it! I just want all the beads to make the most beautiful headband for Camp Fire Girls." Mrs. LaRue took her hand, squeezed it, and assured her she would be first on the list.

When Maggie told Sister that she was going to get the beads from Mrs. LaRue's dress to make a headband, Estelle just smiled and gave her a hug. "Sure you are, honey. That will be very nice." Maggie knew she would keep her secret.

Well, she may not have gotten the very beads from that dress, but one day a package arrived for Maggie from Pennsylvania. In the box were several packages of beads, among them a container of amber sparkling beads, and a small box of brown bugle beads. Maggie almost died of happiness.

After she wrote a nice thank-you note to Mrs. LaRue, she sat down in the craft room with a sheet of graph paper and started to plan her new headband . . . *Let's see, the gold ones will be for the moon and the brown, long ones will be for the tree trunk. Then I will use the green ones for the top of the tree and the blue ones for the river.* She smiled as she planned this special headband, just as special as the pretty lady in Pennsylvania.

CHAPTER 15
The Town Kids and Valentine's Day

"Lana, did you see the sandwiches that Mona had in her lunch yesterday? All the crusts were cut off and she had three different kinds of filling in them!"

"Yeah, I noticed. Also, most of the town kids' moms peel their apples and put them in little sacks like candy comes in."

Maggie thought awhile as she looked out the window of the small bedroom that she, Lana, and Jane shared. "I think I'll ask Miss Haney if I can cut my crusts off and peel my apple." She thought again and decided she would see if her sister would do that for her some day. It would be nice to be more like the town kids now that they had their new bus and could go into town to school. She loved being in a class with so many new people.

"Are there any cute boys in your class, Lana?" Maggie asked. She had skipped third grade, so she was now in fifth grade and beginning to notice the boys from town.

"No, silly, I am just in fourth grade, so I don't even like

boys! Do you?" Maggie rolled her eyes heavenward, sighed, and patted her heart.

"Well, there is this cute red-headed boy in my homeroom, and he smiled at me today."

"So, you didn't answer my question. Do you like him or don'tcha?" Not wanting Lana to tell her brother, Rob, who had liked her for a long time and even had given her his Sunday school envelopes for a present, she answered without her usual enthusiasm.

"Oh, he is just a new friend who smiled at me. But Valentine's Day is coming and I'm gonna erase a name off of one I got last year and give it to him. Don't tell Rob or he'll get mad and won't give me any more presents."

"It's OK 'cause I think he likes a new girl in his class now. Everybody is going crazy with all these new kids they're meeting. Wonder if any of them ever go to the picture show at the same time we do? If they did, maybe you could tell your new friend to meet you there and sit by you. But that means you've got to start minding Miss Haney better, so you can even go to the show. You're always getting on punishment and have to miss the movies."

"Yeah, that would be keen if we just happened to go to the show at the same time and he could sit by me." As she finished her statement, she sighed a big sigh and smiled mysteriously. "I just wonder . . . wouldn't it be fun if we could spend the night in town with a girlfriend who lived close to someone special? But that's out, as you know and I know. No one ever gets to spend the night in town. Nor can anyone spend the night with us, so forget that great idea. I asked Sister why, and she said there were too many of us, and there is only food and bedding for just us, and Miss Haney has her hands full taking care of the twenty-five of us. Shoot!" she said in a pout, as she sat down on her bed to think some more. "There just has to be a way . . . I'll just have to do something about that rule!"

"Like what?" Lana sat on her bed and pretended to be thinking also.

Jane came in about that time and asked what in the world they were thinking about. When Lana told her, she just shook her head. "Forget it! Miss Haney's pet has already asked to

59

spend the night in town, and if the answer was 'no' for her, it is certainly 'no' for us."

"Which pet?" Maggie perked up. She loved to enter into a little friendly gossip about who was doing what and why. In a building of twenty-five girls ('cause she didn't count the two little boys who were just toddlers and stayed in the room across the hall from Miss Haney's room), there was always something to talk about.

"Flossie, of course, silly. She has been her pet ever since she got sick and had to go to that sanitarium out in West Texas for her lungs. When she got back, she acted so pitiful and she doesn't have to do any work."

"Well, if she ever does get to stay in town with a friend, I'm gonna tell Dr. Stanley, as that would not be fair to the rest of us!" Maggie exclaimed as she came right up off her bed, eyes flashing.

"Just simmer down, 'cause it's not gonna happen. You're just getting all riled up for nothing. I think that red-headed boy in town has you acting funny." Lana patted her on the shoulder to settle her down. Maggie started laughing and did a funny little jig to get back in a good mood.

Valentine's Day came, and when their big new bus stopped, all the Home kids piled out, each holding their decorated shoebox with some homemade valentines inside for their classmates. Maggie had one store-bought card, and she had carefully erased the name and painstakingly printed her own name in its place. When she got to her classroom, she was almost out of breath from hurrying and excitement. There on top of her desk was a small chocolate heart wrapped in red cellophane paper. There was no name on it, but when she looked at the boy with red hair, his face was almost the same color as his hair, and he was smiling at her. What a wonderful thing it was that she had a new and special friend. She made sure she put the store-bought card in the decorated box with his name on it. This was the best Valentine's Day ever.

When she opened her lunch sack, she found two different kinds of sandwiches, with the crusts cut off, and her apple had been peeled and wrapped in pretty red cellophane. There was a lovely pink paper heart with a message in red ink that said:

60

"I love you. Your sister, Estelle." There were also two heart-shaped cookies that Sister had helped Miss Haney bake. Maggie's heart was so full it was about to overflow. She would never forget that Valentine's Day—the chocolate heart, the smiling red-headed boy of ten, and the special sandwiches with the crusts cut off . . . just like the town kids.

CHAPTER 16
The Drum and Bugle Corps

When Maggie was twelve years old, she begged Dr. Stanley to allow her to play the snare drum in the Home's drum and bugle corps. He had a man from town coming out to pick several of the kids to play the drums, bugles, bass drum, and cymbals. Everyone was invited to try out. Four girls and four boys were picked for the snare drums, one of which was Maggie. A boy with very good rhythm was chosen to play the bass drum and another boy to play the cymbals. Alex, Maggie's older brother, and two other older kids were picked to play the bugles.

The teacher would come out every week and teach them different pieces of marching music. Maggie dearly loved to beat on her drum, especially when they were taught to do the rim shots. They were getting ready to go to a convention of insurance people in Joplin, Missouri, so they were hard at work.

Dr. Stanley decided that he would let them play at the

Above:
Drum and Bugle Corps. Alex is at top, on left; Maggie on far right, second row from bottom.
Left:
Maggie (bottom row with bandage) and Estelle (top row, middle).

Rotary and Kiwanis lunch meetings in town. Maggie was excited when they marched into the Grayson Hotel for the Kiwanis Club meeting; in fact, she was smiling and having fun beating her snare drum. The boys were dressed in white pants and shirts with purple ties; the girls in white skirts and white blouses with purple ties. All wore little white over-seas hats with green and purple trim, cocked to one side. Maggie wore hers a little to the back so her newly grown-out hair could show. When she finally got to let her bangs grow out, she found waves underneath and loved to comb and fluff her hair. It made her hat sit a little funny, but she felt she had to show off her new hairdo. Her future adoptive father first saw her when she played her drum at his Kiwanis Club.

The drum and bugle corps played at several town events and at a high school PTA meeting. Dr. Stanley was active all over town, and loved to show off his Home kids. By the time summer came, when they played in Joplin, Missouri, they got a standing ovation. Maggie never stopped smiling that whole summer. Every time she closed her eyes during rest hour, she could hear the applause. *Let's see, maybe I could be in a play at school and hear that magic applause again. Or maybe learn to play the saxophone, and play in a band, and people will clap. Or maybe, just maybe, I could learn to tap dance better and . . . and . . .* Maggie went to sleep with a smile on her face.

CHAPTER 17
The Talent Show

The drum and bugle corps, the military drill team, the girl dancers, those who took declamation, and the piano players had certain times of the day, night, and weekends that they met and practiced, all in preparation for performing at the insurance convention in Joplin, Missouri. The date was in July, and each act had to be honed to perfection. Dr. Stanley personally oversaw each and every practice. He alone was the judge and jury, and he was a perfectionist! He planned a big talent show with an audience from town when all the acts were ready.

Maggie played in the drum and bugle corps and also took ballet with a group of girls her age. The teacher came out to the Home from town each Monday night to teach them two specific dances that would require costumes. Poor Miss Haney and a few of the older girls were in charge of making the dance costumes. One dance had the girls dressed as Portuguese peasants, with full skirts, white gypsy blouses, and round circle hats that tied under their chins. A lot of the movements were circles, to the left and to the right. They pointed one toe as they twirled

The Dancers . . . ready to perform. Top photo: Maggie, second from left, and Lana, far right. Bottom photo: Jane, at far left, with Maggie and Lana fourth and fifth in line.

one way, and the other toe when they twirled the other way. Maggie had a little trouble keeping up with which way to turn. The teacher, Miss Millie, finally stopped the rest of the group and worked with only Maggie. One hand was on the waist, the other over the head, one toe was pointing, and all the while, twirling. It was almost too much for a young girl who was a lot more comfortable climbing trees down at the park. Maggie also had a little speech to learn called "Multiplication Table," but that was not as hard as dancing. She dearly loved to beat the drum in the drum and bugle corps.

The military drill was something that had to do with the Woodmen Circle Lodge's ritual. Maggie had been doing this since she was seven, and now she was thirteen and knew it by heart. There were four main posts—north, south, east and west. Each post had a name, and older ladies of the lodge held these four positions. There were ten girls and ten boys, dressed all in white with capes that were half green and half purple. A cute girl from town played the march on the piano, and the twenty boys and girls did some fancy maneuvers as they marched to the snappy music. Ladies of the lodge came out from town to go through the routine with the boys and girls before the national officers of the insurance company came to their board meetings at the Home. The drill team would escort each one of the national officers, who resided, at least part time, in Omaha, Nebraska, to the four different posts. The leader of the drill team had a whistle, and all commands were given by the tooting of the whistle. Oh, how Maggie wanted to be the one who tooted that whistle! But just like never getting to become the Virgin Mary in the Christmas pageant, she never got to toot that command whistle. This was all very serious stuff.

The poem was easier for her, as she could do that alone, and no one knew if she messed up. She loved the little poem that Dr. Stanley taught her. He knew she would give it a lot of expression. She would stand up very straight, clear her throat, and look all around the room to make sure she had everyone's attention, straighten her dress, take a deep breath and begin:

The Multiplication Table
(Author unknown)

I studied my tables over and over,
And backward and forward too,
But I couldn't remember 6x9,
And I didn't know what to do.

'Til Sister told me to play with my doll,
And not to bother my head.
If you call her your dear little Fifty-four
You'll learn it by heart, she said.

So I called her my dear little Fifty-four
A thousand times 'til I knew
The answer to six times nine
As well as the answer of two times two.

Next day Elizabeth Wigglesworth,
Who always looked so proud,
Said six times nine was sixty-four,
And I nearly laughed out loud.

But I wished I hadn't
When teacher said:
"Now Maggie, tell if you can . . ."
I thought of my doll, and sakes alive,
I answered: "Mary Ann."

When Maggie got to the part, "Next day Elizabeth Wigglesworth . . .," she would put her nose in the air and act very snooty. Then at the end when she did the part about "I thought of my doll," she would roll her eyes to heaven, take her hands from her hips to her head, and very dramatically say: "I answered: 'Mary Ann.'" She loved the applause, and there was always applause.

The drum and bugle corps was getting better and better and were asked to go to different lunch clubs and meetings to perform. They were always applauded, and again, Maggie and all the others enjoyed the attention. Her brother, Alex, had graduated from high school and was going to college, as were Katy and Sally, so they had to be replaced by three other trum-

Home kids with grandmas and grandpas (retired members). Alex is standing, fourth from left; Mick and Maggie in middle, with Estelle in checked dress.

peters, who were not quite as good. But they were loud, and that was good, as the snare drummers were *really* loud.

July came, and all the kids, the cute girl from town who played the piano for the drill team, Dr. and Mrs. Stanley, Miss Haney, and the mother of the town girl boarded the Katy Train that was to take them to Joplin, Missouri. It was some job, not only getting all the children aboard but also all of the musical instruments, the dance costumes, the white uniforms, and the all the trunks. The grown-ups were very hot and tired and cross, all patience gone. The kids were too excited and could not be quiet. After all, none of them had been on a train before. After two or three hard looks, they began to settle down.

Maggie was so upset when her beloved Mick ran to sit by the town girl who played the piano. Her mother let him squeeze in between them, and she sat somewhere else later on. Dr. Stanley finally separated them because Mick was holding her hand and looking moon-eyed at her. Maggie smiled as she looked out the window at the flashing scenery, thinking to herself, *It isn't going to be such a bad trip after all . . .*

All of their performances at the national convention were big hits, and the ladies from all over the United States pinched their cheeks, gave them bosom-hugs, and told them how adorable they were. All in all their "talent show" had been a big hit, and even Dr. Stanley told them: "Well done, boys and girls!"

After they boarded the train to go back home, Maggie put her head on Sister's shoulder, closed her eyes, and murmured more to herself than to Estelle . . . *Maybe, just maybe, someday Mick will hold my hand and smile at me the way he did at . . . what's-her-name . . .* Sister leaned closer to hear what she was saying, but Maggie was asleep, smiling.

CHAPTER 18
A Special Sunday

Maggie stayed dressed in her Sunday school clothes every Sunday. Even after lunch, she stayed dressed, just knowing in her heart each week that her daddy or her uncle would surely come to visit. Uncle Ted did come once soon after they arrived at the Home and brought each of them a bright pink peanut patty, remembering it was their favorite candy. He made sure they were all right, then headed on to Oklahoma to help with harvesting wheat. He said he'd try to come back, maybe on a Sunday. He told them that their daddy was probably helping with the harvest, maybe even in Kansas. Maggie was sure each Sunday that one of them would come to visit them, and maybe, just maybe, take them back to their grandfather's home in West Texas. Estelle and Alex never stayed dressed, as they knew that no one was coming, but they did not say anything to Maggie. Finally, Alex got permission to meet with both of his sisters and to have a serious talk with them. They met at the red and white brick pergola, their favorite secret place.

"Girls, I have been giving something a lot of thought, and even though it will hurt your feelings, I think it is time for you to know the truth. Uncle Ted wrote some time ago that he and his wife were having another baby, and it was out of the question for them to take us back to live with them. Now, as far as our daddy is concerned, no one seems to know where he is. He did some harvesting across Oklahoma and Kansas, but seems to have disappeared. I don't think we should look for him, as it has been five years that we have been here, and a year before that since we saw him last.

"I am going to graduate soon and will be leaving to go to SMU in Dallas on a band scholarship. You can be assured that I will always come back to be with you girls at holidays and in the summer. But there is only our daddy's sister, Aunt Ina, to visit you, and she has moved to Arizona, and probably won't be able to come back again. We just need to know that the three of us will always see each other, no matter what, or how many miles separate us." He put his arm around each of his sisters, hugged them tightly, and then they all three stood and had a group hug.

From that day on, Maggie changed her Sunday school clothes as soon as lunch was over, and tried not to notice the family members who came to see some of the other children. She made a dash from the Big Building to the girls' building to change clothes and lie on her bed to read a good book. *Who cares if no one comes to see me? I couldn't care less! I would just have to tell them goodbye again, and who wants to do that, over and over? Judy and Jo cry their eyes out every week when their mother has to go back to Fort Worth to work. Who needs that? Not me! That's for sure!* Maggie would start to read, but would end up staring out the window, blinking to hold back the tears.

One Sunday was different. A man in town who liked the way she played the snare drums at his luncheon club brought his wife to meet Maggie. One of the older girls, Sally, came quietly to her bed and said that a Mr. and Mrs. Boyd had come to see her.

"Who in the world are they?" she asked as she started putting on the Sunday clothes she had just hung up.

"Someone you met last week at Dr. Stanley's luncheon club when you played in the drum and bugle corps there."

"Oh! I remember that nice man. He really liked the way I

smiled when I beat the drum. He seemed real nice and friend-ly. Goody! Someone has come to visit ME! Wow! Wait 'til I tell Sister and Brother!"

"They want to meet your sister also. Dr. Stanley thought that it would be easier for you that way."

"That sweet Pappy. I'll just have to give him a big hug next time I see him! I'll run and rush Sister. Maybe they'll take us into town to get some ice cream!"

She was almost to the stairs leading down when Estelle came from her room, smiling and holding out her arms to Maggie. "Won't this be fun, sweetie? You must be on your very best behavior."

The two girls walked quickly to the living room, where visiting was done. Sure enough, there was the nice man, and she presumed that the lady with him was his wife. He put a protective arm around each girl's shoulder and turned to his wife, his crystal blue eyes sparkling.

"Nettie, this is the little girl, Maggie, I told you about, and this must be her sister. Ah, I'm sorry, I asked Dr. Stanley your name, but I have forgotten it."

"It's Estelle, and it means 'Little Star,'" Maggie quickly said, as she knew her sister was very shy. But Estelle motioned to the sofa and asked if the Boyds would like to sit down and visit. Maggie was shocked, but took the man's hand and led him there. The nice lady was shy also, and took Estelle's hand as they followed. After chatting a minute, the lady asked if they could have a tour of the girls' building since they had only been in the Big Building.

"Sure you can," said Maggie. She pulled on the man to get up and follow her as she skipped along pointing to the different rooms. In a quiet voice, and walking nicely, Estelle motioned to the room on the left and told them that it was the music room. "Some of the older girls play the piano for us to sing hymns at our morning devotions, and sometimes Pappy Stanley plays and we sing 'Watermelon, Watermelon,'" Maggie chirped happily.

"And this is my favorite room, well almost, next to the dining room, 'cause this is where we get our books to read. It is also where we have to study when school is going on, every night! Ugh!"

"Maggie, you know you like to study." Sister cut her eyes at Maggie as if to say: "Watch your step, young lady." Ignoring the look, Maggie told them it was a library-study room, but she liked all the books there on the shelves better than her school books. For sure! Mr. Boyd grinned and gave his wife a little nudge.

Then Estelle showed them the other end of the hall, where the sewing room, dining room, kitchen and pantry were located. These were her favorite rooms, she explained quietly, as she loved to sew and cook. Maggie just rolled her eyes heavenward and laughingly said, "Not me!" Mr. Boyd laughed too, and ruffled her shiny, brown, curly hair. "I'll bet that's the truth, honey." Her eyes became as large as silver dollars as she was not used to being called "honey." *That must mean he likes me,* she thought to herself, and took his hand again.

"How would you girls like to go into town to Ashburn's and get some ice cream?" he asked, smiling.

"Yes, yes, yes!" Maggie sang out as she danced around and around, clapping her hands.

"Maggie!" Sister said in her sternest voice, which really was not very mean at all. "Just settle down, while I go to ask Miss Haney." She disappeared down a little back hall off the kitchen and upstairs to the housemother's room. She came back down and asked if Dr. Stanley had given permission when they talked to him earlier, at the Big Building. Mr. Boyd shook his head up and down and smiled at both girls. Mrs. Boyd nodded, but did not smile very much, and when the girls got into their car to go into town, they found out why.

"Girls, before we go, there is something I want to say. We lost our only little girl a year ago with a kidney disease. It has been very hard for us, and also very lonely. That is why we came to visit, as we miss our little girl, and we know you must miss your mother and father also. Maybe we can cheer each other up." Mrs. Boyd reached in her purse for a white handkerchief with lace trim, and dabbed at the tears that began to fall.

"I am so sorry," Estelle said as she reached from the back seat and patted the lady's shoulder. She knew well how it felt to lose someone you loved.

"Me, too," Maggie said, patting Mr. Boyd's shoulder. Luckily they had reached the ice cream place, and Maggie started to get excited. "I wonder what flavor I would like the best. What flavor do you like, Mr. Boyd?"

"Well, honey, I really like Hawaiian Delight, which is mainly pineapple with little bits of fruit in it. Oh, and also coconut. Do you want to join me and try a cone of Hawaiian Delight? How about you, Estelle?"

"That sounds good to me," Maggie said in her cheerful way. "Mrs. Boyd, what do you like the best?"

"I think I'll have the fresh peach. And Estelle, how about you? Will you join me and try the peach?"

Estelle was still sad from hearing about their little girl, but agreed to have the peach cone.

On the way back to the Home, Mr. Boyd took a turn off the road and went to a part of town where some new houses were being built. All of a sudden, they were sitting in front of a sweet little white frame house with a big round window. The Boyds told them that they were building this home, and the window was called a bay window. The house sat at the top of the hill and was the very first house being built on that street. They all got out of the car to look inside the unfinished house. There were big trees on the lot, and Mr. Boyd said that he was planning a rose garden in the middle of the backyard in the shape of a diamond. Both girls thought everything looked a little like their grandfather's home back in West Texas. Mrs. Boyd noticed a sadness and said it was time for them to get the girls back before someone thought they had been kidnapped. She smiled at both girls. So did he.

When they got back to the girls' building, they both thanked the Boyds, and Maggie gave them both a hug. Estelle was halfway up the sidewalk when Maggie caught up with her. She skipped backwards in front of her sister and took her hand.

"Wasn't that fun! And that ice cream was so good! Was your peach yummy?" she asked, as she danced in a circle until she was dizzy.

"Yes, sweetie, it was really good, and they are such nice people. Mrs. Boyd seemed so sad, though. Poor thing. Just think, to have your only little girl die. Mr. Boyd does not seem as sad, or he just hides it better, don't you think?"

"They are like you and me, I guess. I cover up my sadness by acting happy and silly, but you are more like the lady, and the sadness shows. But always remember, Sister, we still have each other and Brother." With that bit of philosophy over and done with, she ran up the stairs ahead of her sister to tell of their great adventure. It was Sunday, and they had company, and had been to town! *So what if it wasn't their daddy or their uncle! Who cared? That Hawaiian Delight ice cream cone was the very best in the whole world!*

"Hey Judy," Maggie called to her friend, "guess where we've been? There is this really nice couple in town, who lost their little girl, and they took us to get ice cream. It was called Hawaiian Delight and it had pineapple, and . . ." her happy voice faded as she went up the stairs to finish telling of her special Sunday. Estelle watched her go and felt sad, yet glad. She knew in her heart that Maggie would someday have a real home, and that little white cottage at the top of the hill might just be it.

CHAPTER 19

Goodbye

Maggie stood on the steps of the Big Building and waved goodbye to all of the exes from the Home. They had spent almost the entire day looking through all the desolate and decaying rooms with disbelief and even tears. The halls that used to shine like glass were now covered with dust and trash from vandals who had broken in and caused havoc. The grand old dining room with waxed, oak floors sustained the most damage. The floors were warped from the casement windows being broken, allowing the rain to pour in. The most non-caring person or persons in the world had made a fire right on the oak floor, and a huge hole had burned through to the basement.

They all shook their heads, remembering the room where they had all their Sunday lunches and holiday meals together. The marble fireplace, which was always a cheerful backdrop for the great, green tree at Christmas, had graffiti sprayed all over it. Someone had to be drunk or crazy on drugs to have left such horror, in a room where "Silent Night" was once sung so sweetly.

The "Big Building," Pergola and The Gate (after thirty years of neglect).

Why hadn't someone guarded these hallowed halls? Ownership had changed hands several times, and it was obvious some of the developers did not care, as the buildings were all in good external repair when the Home closed in 1970. There was no chance now to restore it to its original grandeur. The present owner was at least trying to cut down some of the weeds and overgrown shrubbery, and chain the two gates.

It was decided that when Maggie took back the key to the real estate agent, she would tell him that it was beyond their joint means to buy the property in its present condition. They agreed, however, that the agent should suggest to the owner that movie companies in the Dallas and Austin area be contacted, as it would be a good property for movies to be made there. Maggie was putting many of their remembered stories into a book, and perhaps her book could become a movie. It would surely be different from the Jane Eyre-type orphanage.

All went back to the Big Building, momentarily sad, as they knew they may not see the old buildings or perhaps each other for many years, maybe never. As the last car went out the gate, Maggie kept smiling and waving. When she turned to lock the weather-beaten oak door with boards covering the sides, where leaded glass used to sparkle and shine like a thousand diamonds, shocked, she found there were tears on her cheeks. Since unhappiness was not her natural state, she quickly brushed the tears away and rushed down the front steps, leaving behind the ghosts who lingered there.

She quickly got into her car and drove toward the east entrance gate, as the west exit gate was still locked. She stopped in the driveway outside the gate and locked the chain that had been unsuccessful in keeping out vandals. Closing her eyes one last time, she again could smell the lilacs that once bloomed there. She also thought she could hear the gleeful laughter of children playing hide-and-go-seek.

Maggie drove to the highway, took one quick look back, and waved a final goodbye.

**Class of 1942
Sherman High School
Class Favorites**

*Photos taken 1941 (the
year Maggie was adopted)*

*Mick O'Brian
Most Handsome Boy*

*Maggie
Most Representative Girl*

Epilogue

Maggie was adopted when she was fifteen. The Home was not an adopting home, but more like a permanent babysitting place, where the children could be left until their next of kin could come and get them. Since Maggie's next of kin was her missing father, she had to go to court and testify that she had not seen nor heard from him since she entered the Home at age six. She was asked if she would like to become Mr. and Mrs. Boyd's daughter. She shook her head up and down, looked at the Boyds, smiled, then told the judge: "Yes, sir. That would be wonderful."

Her guardianship papers had already been signed by her sister, Estelle, as her brother, Alex, was overseas with the air force in the Pacific theater. Estelle had not wanted to give up being Maggie's guardian, but knew she would have more advantages with this nice couple who had lost their only little girl. Estelle knew her little sister could bring them joy.

The Boyds had to agree to send Maggie to college, and Estelle knew she would not be able to do that. Also, she was to visit Maggie as much as she liked, and Maggie could visit her. Estelle was working at the home office of the insurance company that suported the Home. She lived in one room in a boardinghouse, and she knew the Boyds planned to give Maggie her own room in their little white cottage. They came to the Home for three years before Estelle was old enough to become her guardian. She also had to get Alex's permission, and that took time, as he was in the midst of a war.

Maggie was lonely at first, but soon made good friends in her neighborhood. There were a lot of adjustments to be made, but they did give each other some happiness that they would not have had otherwise. Two granddaughters and three great-granddaughters were icing on the cake. They made the difference.

Mick O'Brian, and all of the boys at the Home who were old enough, enlisted in one of the branches of the service. Mick joined the navy, and while stationed in California he made friends with a boy from Ohio. Although Maggie wrote several of the boys, she wrote Alex and Mick the most. Her childhood crush on Mick turned into a friendship that would last a lifetime. He introduced her to Bob, his best buddy from Ohio, by letter. They all wrote back and forth for three years, and when the war ended, Mick invited Bob to visit him at the Home and to meet Maggie. A year later, Mick was Bob's best man at his and Maggie's wedding. Maggie had graduated from college by then and was going to work for Eastern Airlines in Houston.

After she met Bob, Houston was history. They had two daughters, two sons-in-law, and three granddaughters. All happily live in the Dallas area. The friendship with the O'Brian boys and their families has lasted a lifetime, especially the bond between Mick and Bob, due to fighting with the 4th Marine Division during WWII. Maggie still teases Mick about how he paid the boys in the band to take her off his hands at the dance where she wore the infamous red dress. He always denies her accusations. He and Bob tell the same funny war stories every time they get together to play golf. They talk about the fun things that happened, never the serious. They were together on Saipan and Iwo Jima, but only in later years were these battles mentioned.

Maggie wrote Bob about imaginary dates they were having and even sent him little swatches of the color dress she

Top:
The Boyds adopted Maggie when she was fifteen.
Left:
Maggie, Alex and Estelle in Omaha, Nebraska, for Estelle's formal wedding.
Alex gave Estelle away. Maggie was maid of honor.
Below:
Maggie and Bob's wedding. Mick O'Brian (fifth from left) was his best man. Estelle was not there due to the birth of her second daughter. Alex was teaching.

wore. She also kept both of them posted as to the "Hit Parade's Top Ten," which were the top ten popular music hits each week. Sometimes she even wrote the words, especially *I'll Be Seeing You*. Bob always said her letters took the sting out of the subversive messages they received in the Pacific from Tokyo Rose.

Finally, Maggie worked through her bitterness toward her father. She saw him while she and Alex were attending the University of Texas at Austin. Alex had arranged the meeting without telling her, so when the office called that her father was out front, she happily went, thinking she was about to see her adoptive father. A stranger came toward her and said he was Cliff, her father, and told her how much she looked like her mother. Maggie told him he was not her father, and that she had waited for him for fifteen years, but he never came. She now had a father and mother who cared for her, and he had given up that right. She turned and walked back into the office, shaking. She never saw him again.

Recently, Maggie attended Richland Community College and took a wellness class in creative writing. A wonderful teacher led the class of diverse ages through life experiences. Eventually, she helped each one find the story beneath the story and how to find release by writing about it.

One night Maggie started to write in her journal, and in no time completed a story about a little girl called Maggie. She had lost not only her mother, aunt, grandmother, and grandfather from disease and natural causes in one year, but also her father, who just went away after her mother's funeral. She told of her sadness, and anger, and that she buried him so deep she made herself never think of him. Her story ended by her realizing that the short note of forgiveness she had written him, at his request, when he was dying of cancer, was not sincere.

Maggie prayed and prayed and finally decided what she needed to do. She had read that in Indian folklore the Indians wrote symbols on birch bark, things that troubled them, and floated them down the river. This released them from that worry. Maggie, now many years later, knew of a little stream where she could leave her message in a shell and let it drift away. She found her prettiest mother-of-pearl shell and wrote

Maggie, Estelle, and Alex's father, who just disappeared after their Mother's funeral.

Mother of Maggie, Estelle, and Alex (died in 1930).

these words in permanent purple ink: "Father, I forgive you." As the shell floated away, she cried.

She went to class the next day and turned in her term paper called "Forgiveness." The teacher wrote Maggie a note when she returned her graded notebook: "You have been an inspiration to us all as we watched you deal so deeply with your oldest and most powerful pain, and you showed us how to forgive and release."

Maggie received an "A" in the course, but her biggest reward was the weight that was lifted from her heart.

Maggie and her family today.

About the Author

Margery Evans Eldridge was born in Ralls, Texas, in 1925. After the death of most of their family, she and her sister and brother (Frances and Don) were taken to Sherman, Texas, to spend several years at the Woodmen Circle Home. The Home was owned and sponsored by the Supreme Forest Woodmen Circle Life Insurance Company.

In 1941 she was adopted from her sister and brother, as they had become her guardians, with permission from the Insurance Board of Directors. Mr. and Mrs. Boyd Evans of Sherman adopted her on October 26, 1941. Margery was fifteen and a junior at Sherman High School when she was adopted. She graduated in 1942.

Margery attended Austin College in Sherman for two years and graduated from the University of Texas at Austin in 1945, with a B.A. in English and minor in philosophy. She worked in Sherman for two years, then married Robert H. Eldridge, of Springfield, Ohio. They have two daughters, Lisa Eldridge Grinsfelder and Kimberly Eldridge South, and three granddaughters, Julie and Emily Grinsfelder, and Meridith South.

The author is a retired schoolteacher, and for a time created custom flower designs for decorators in the Dallas area. She takes computer and creative writing courses at Richland Community College and still enjoys learning.